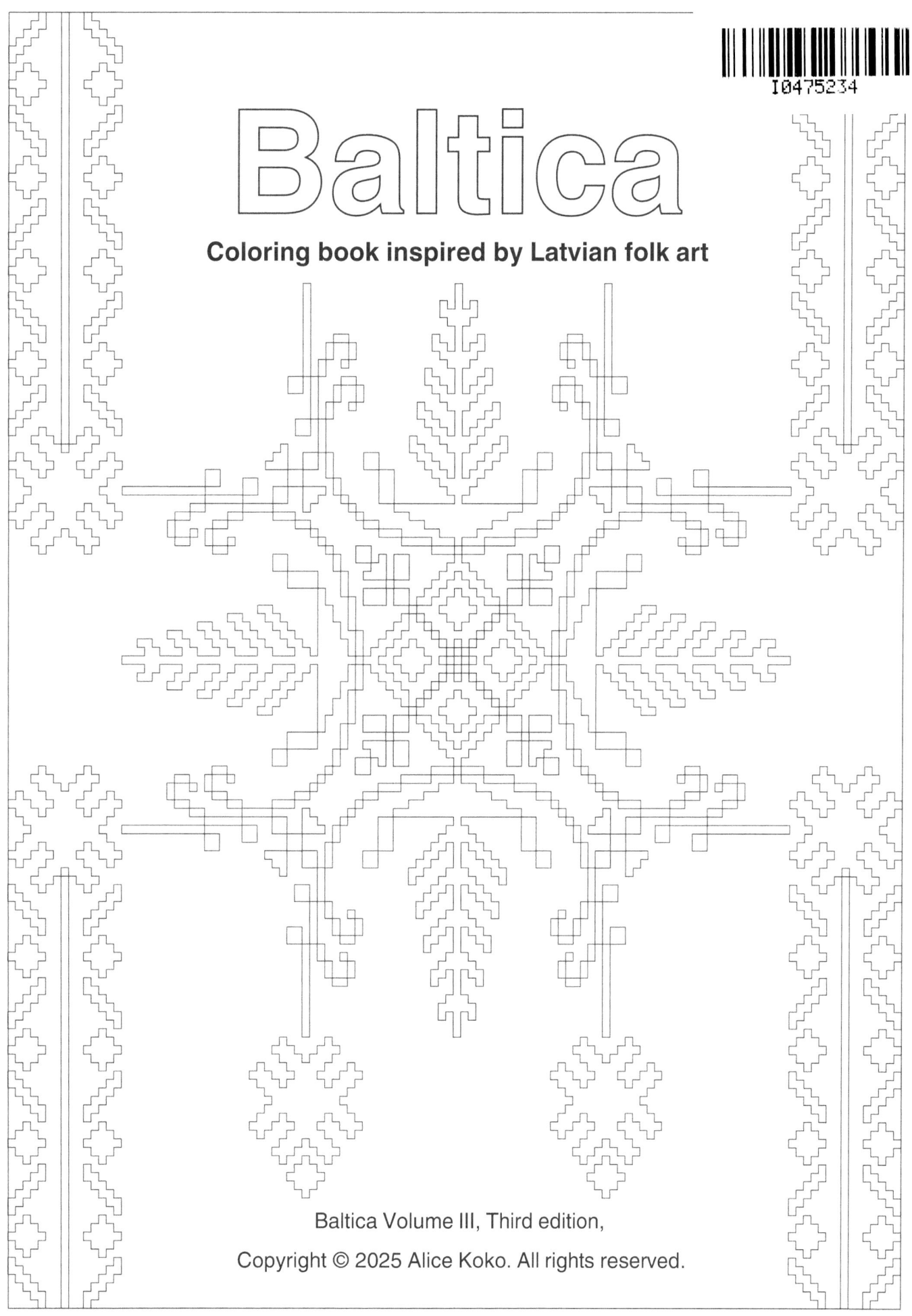

Baltica

Coloring book inspired by Latvian folk art

I0475234

Baltica Volume III, Third edition,

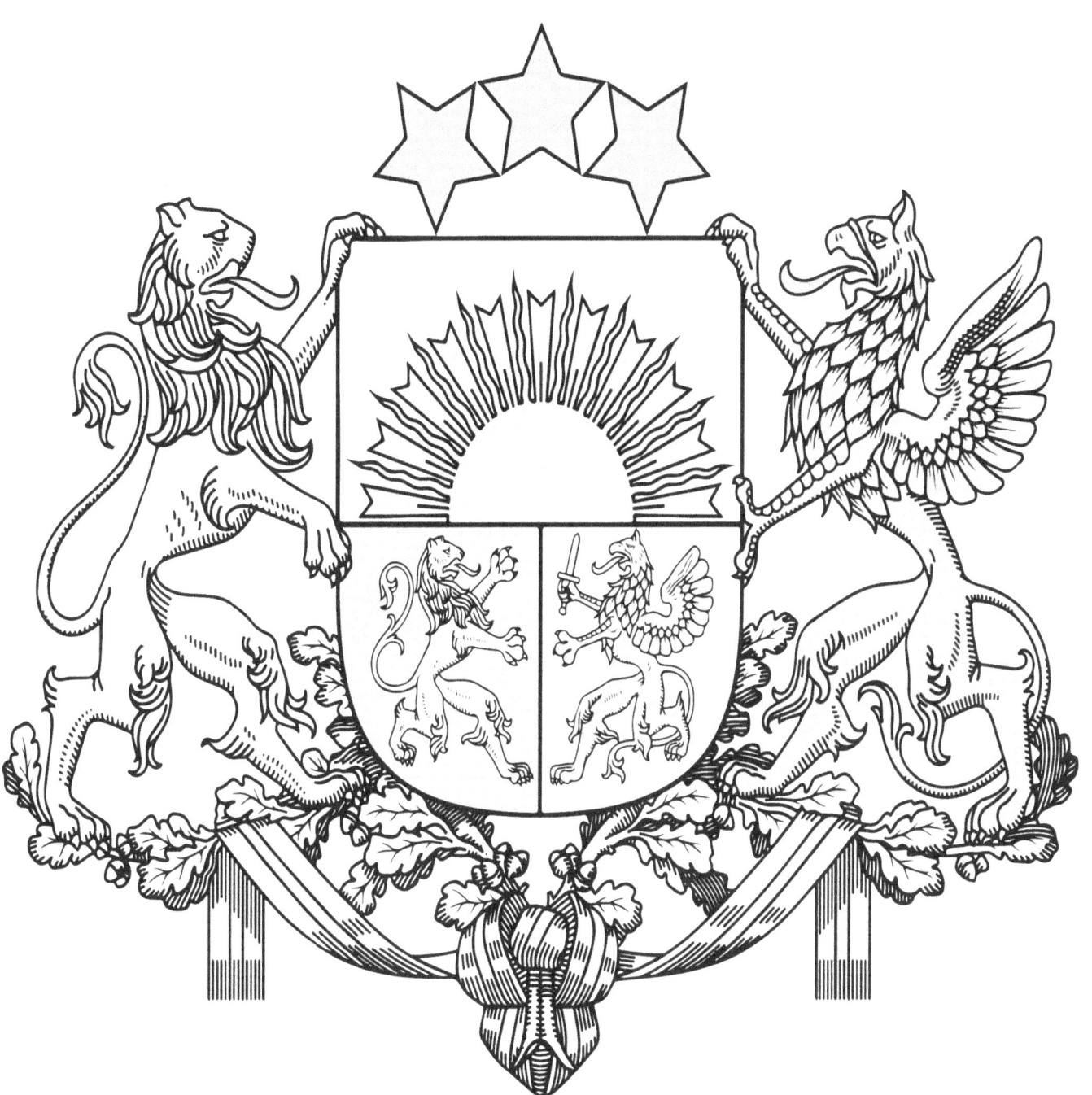

Latvia is a Baltic state in northern Europe; it is bordered by Estonia to the north,
Lithuania to the south, Russia to the east and Belarus to the southeast,
coastline of the Baltic Sea as well maritime border to the west alongside Sweden.
It's landscape is marked by wide beaches on the shores of Baltic Sea that
stretches 500 km and dense, sprawling forests that cover more than half of the country.
It is situated on a trading crossroads and has served as a bridge between
Western Europe and Russia for centuries. Riga is the capital of Latvia.
Riga's Old town is a UNESCO heritage site as well Art Nouveau capital of the world.
It is considered the "Paris of the North."
Latvia is renowned for its masterful craftsmanship and beautiful folk art in textiles,
embroidery and knitwear. Handicraft traditions are honored and passed on
for generations. Here's a little glimpse into the beauty of the Latvian folk art.
Enjoy!

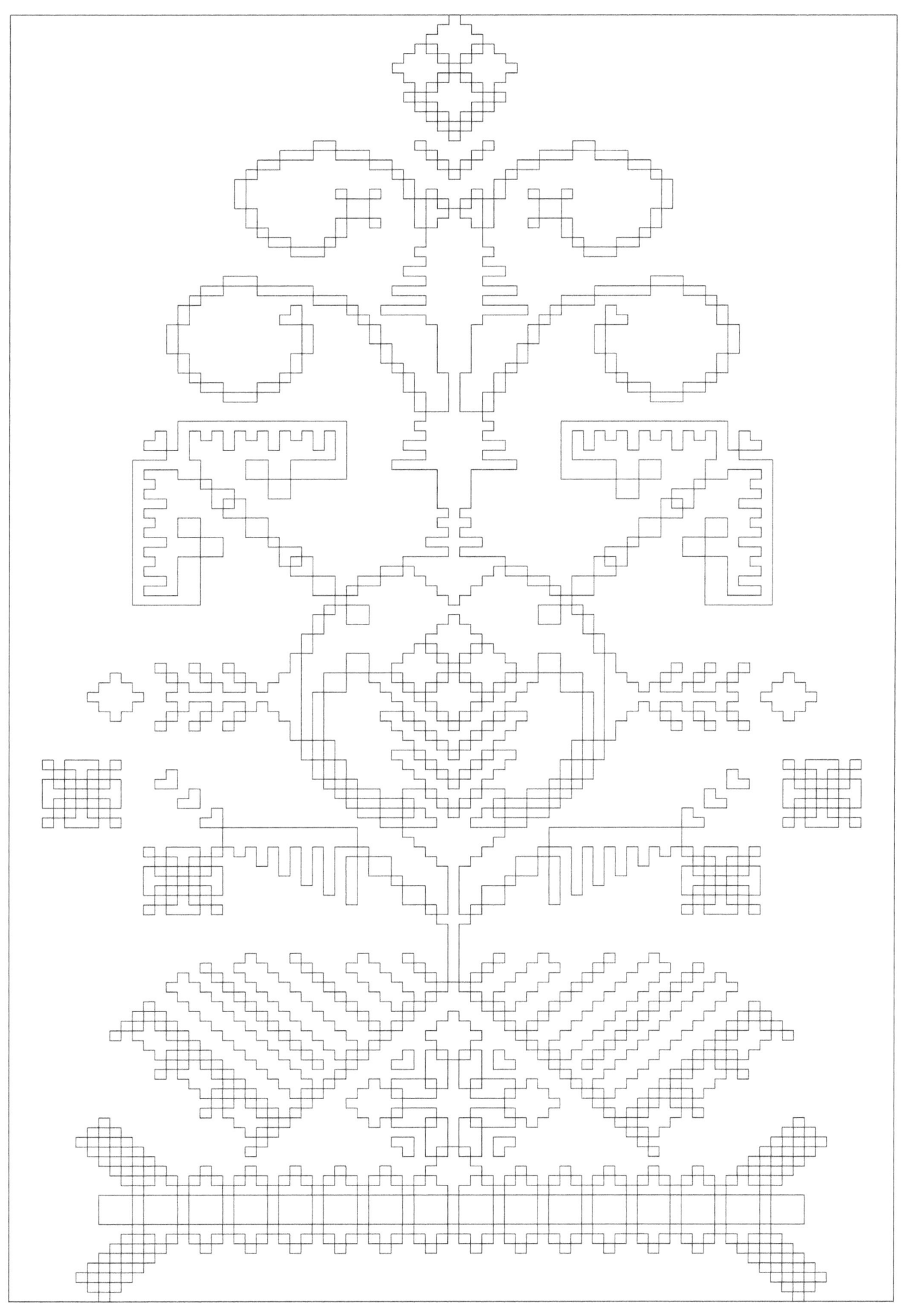

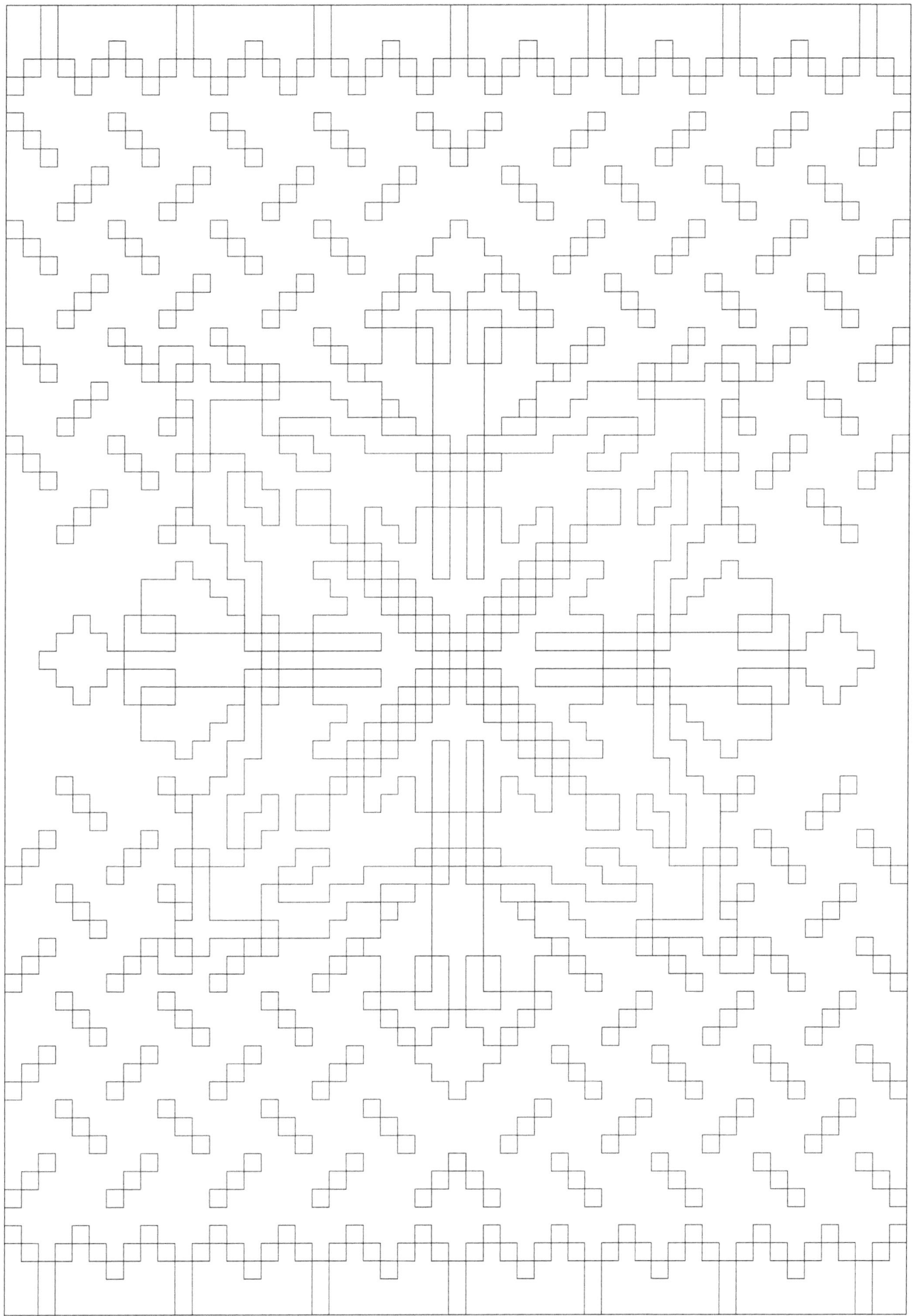

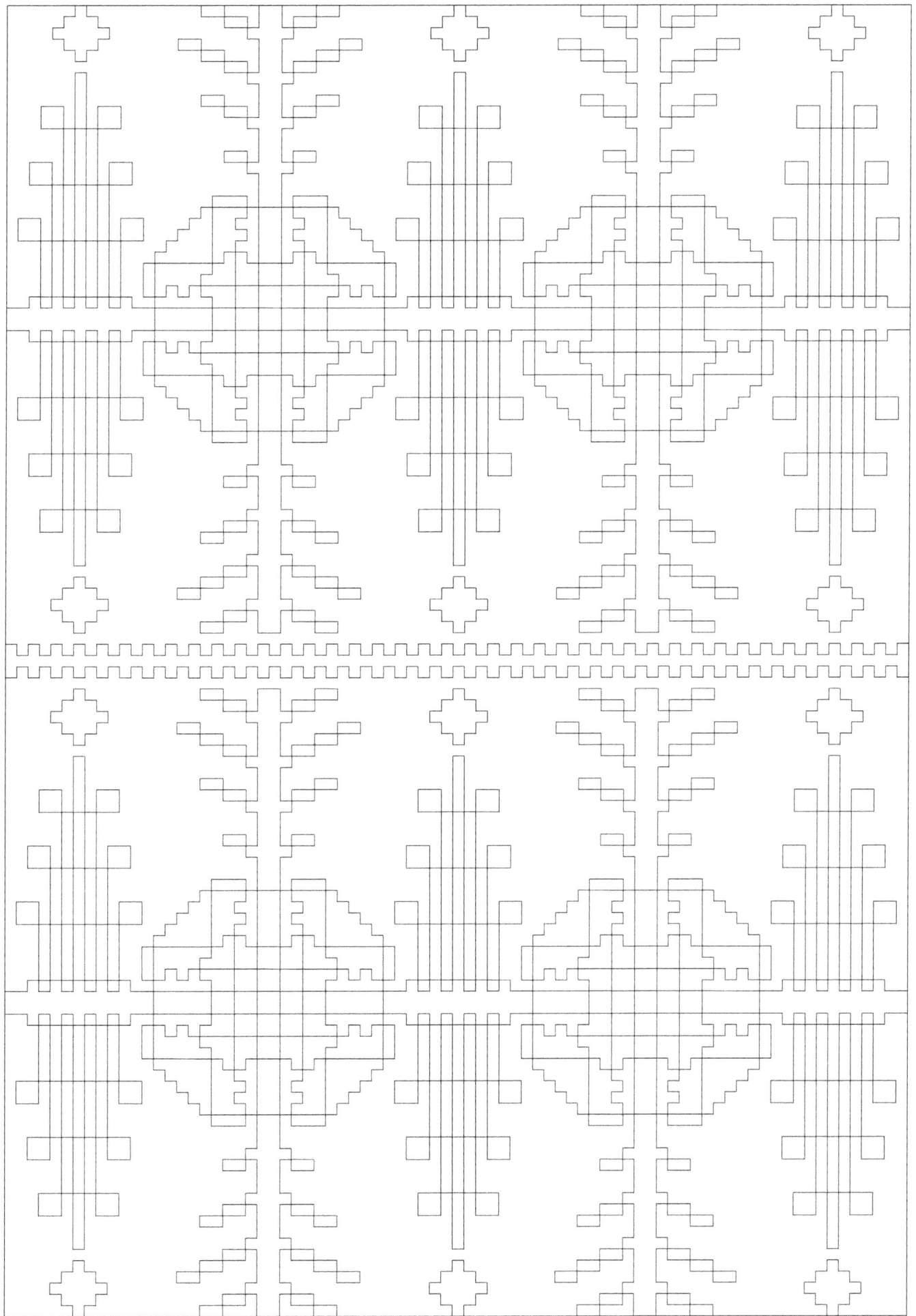

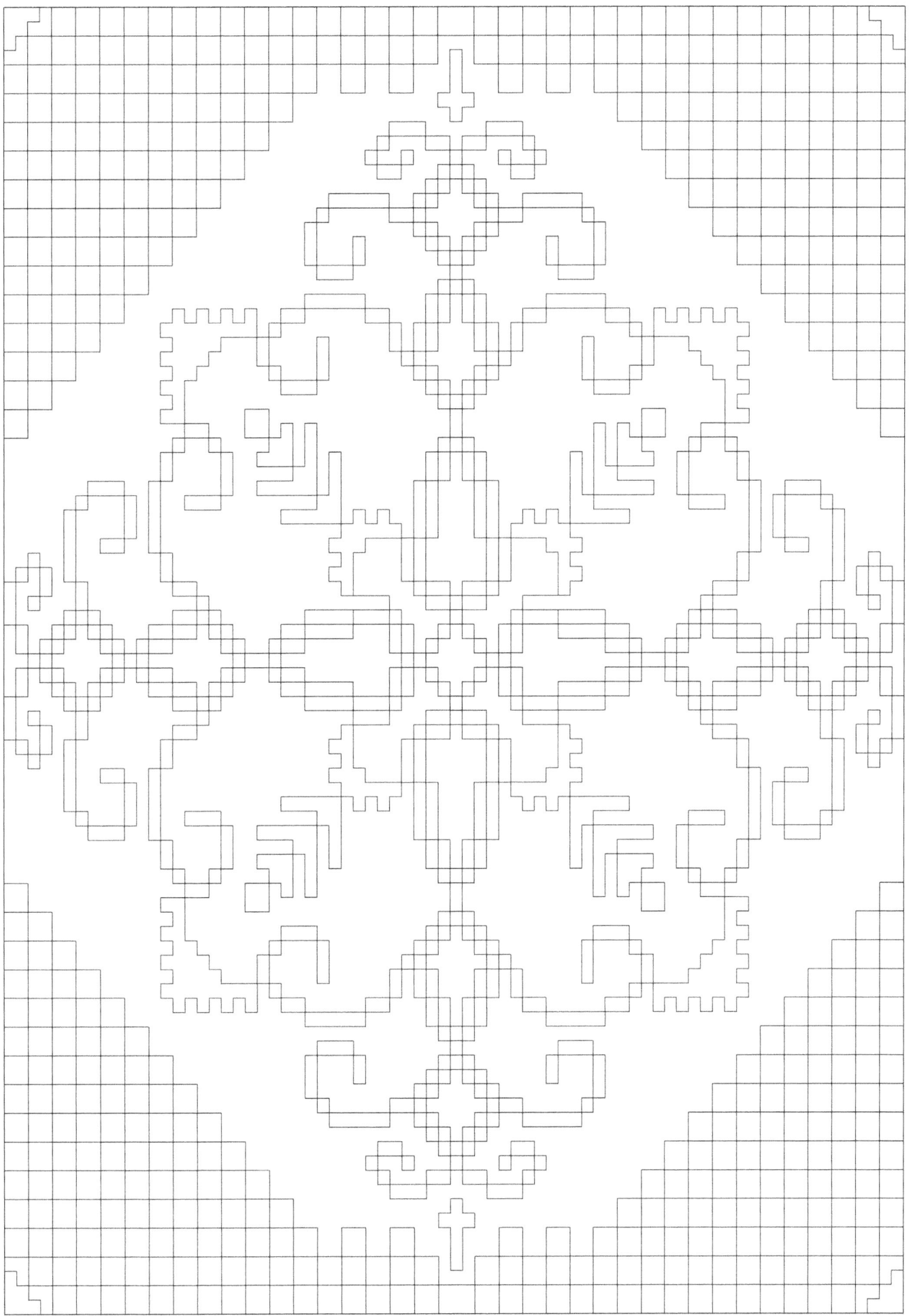

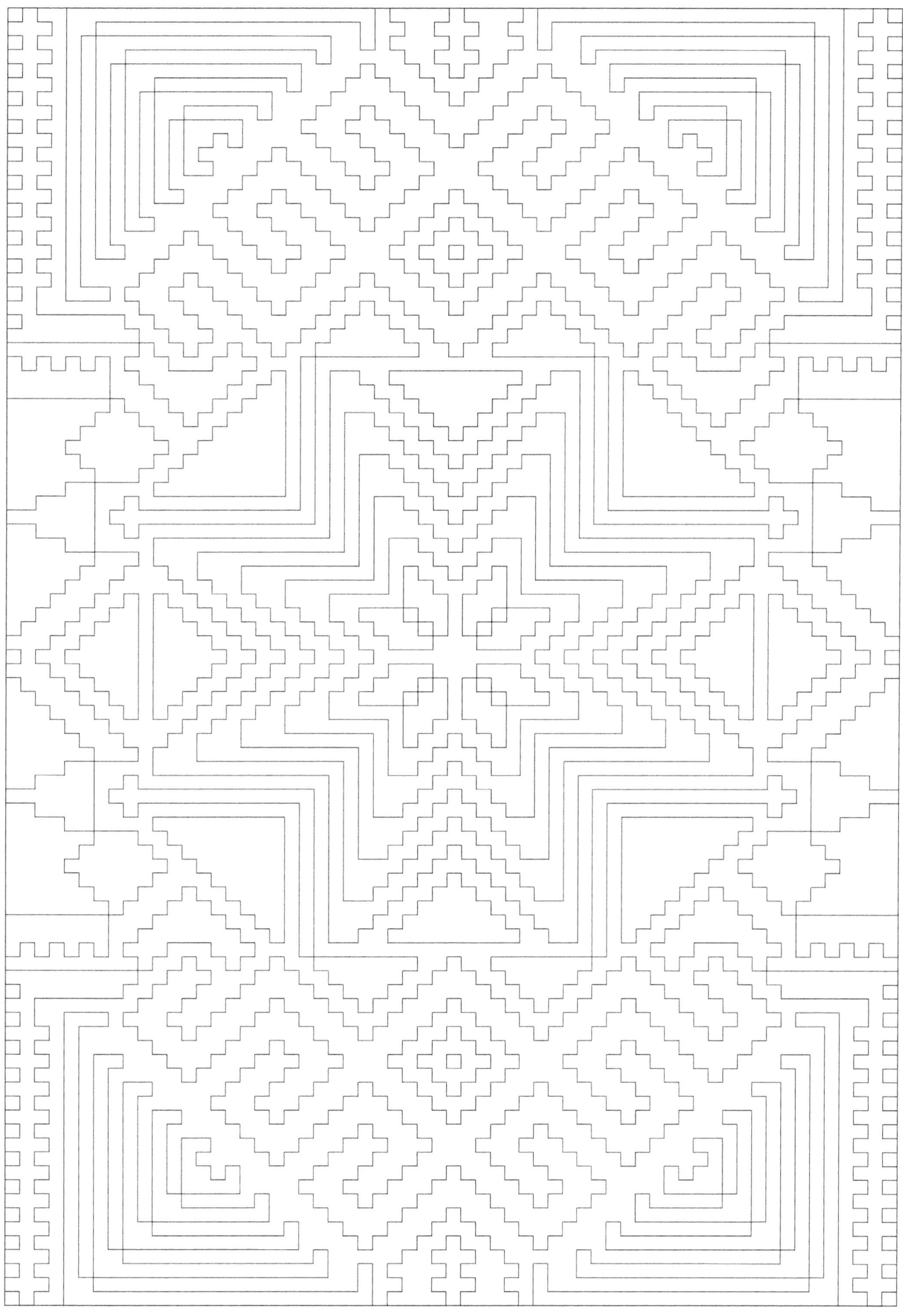

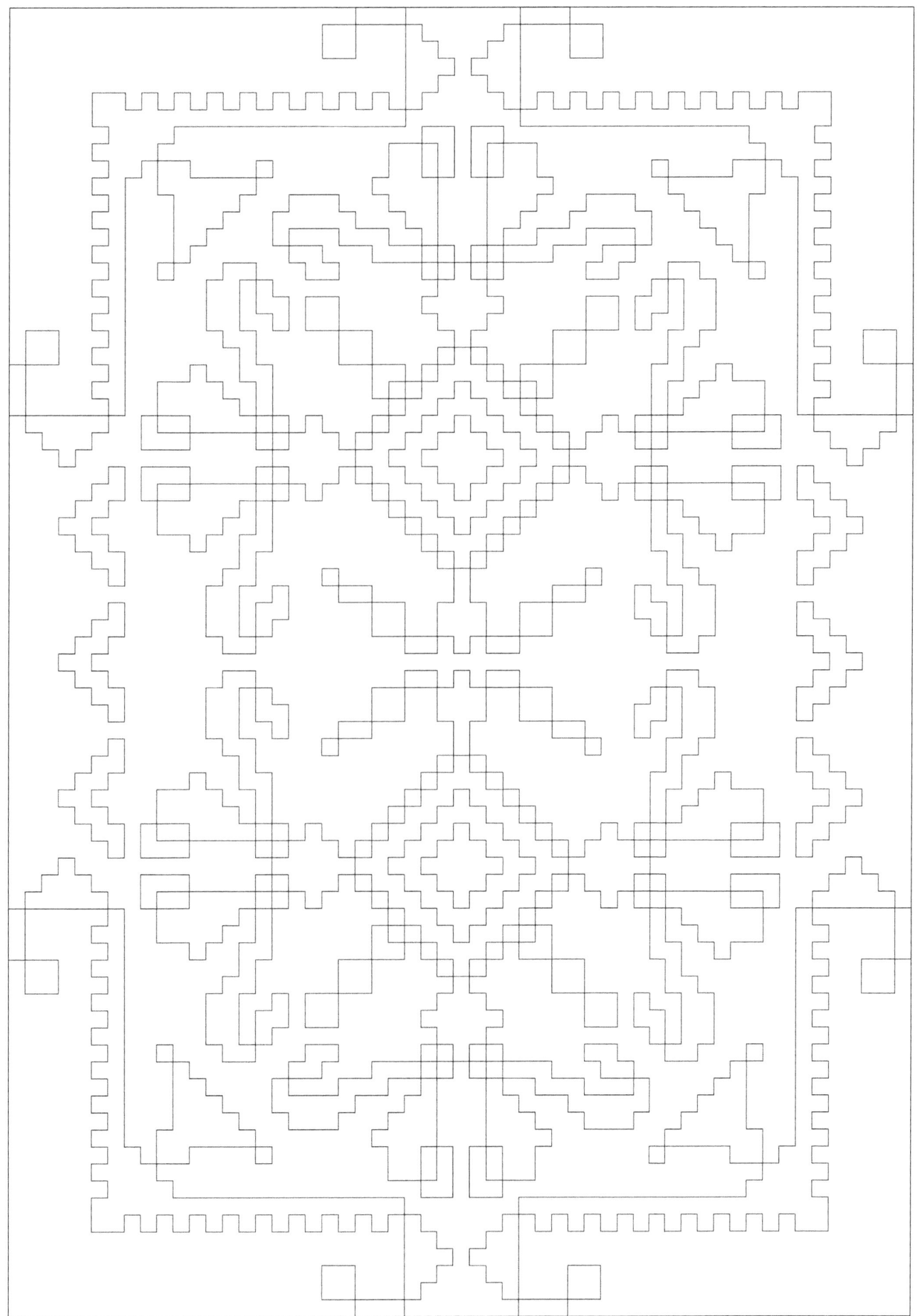

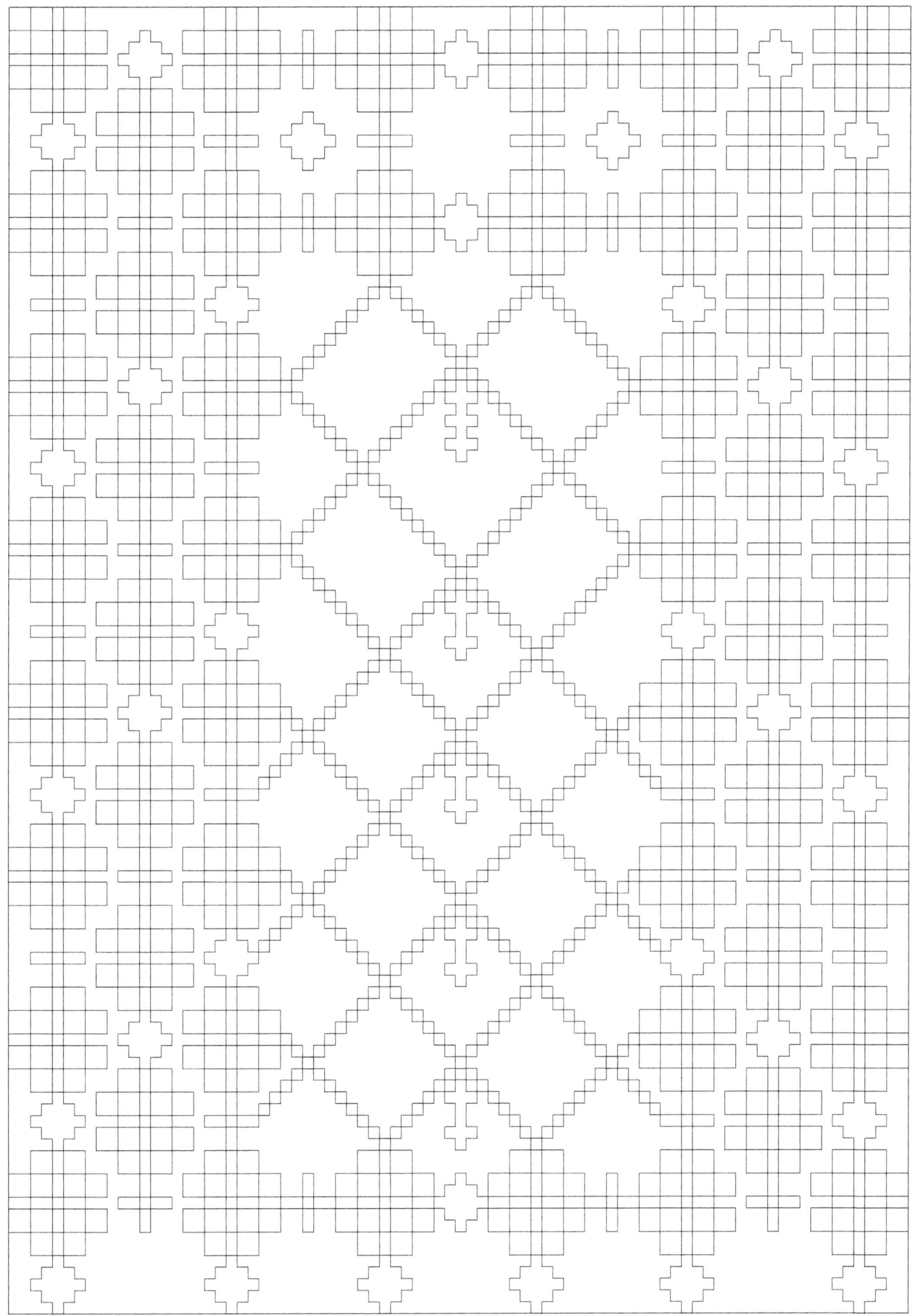

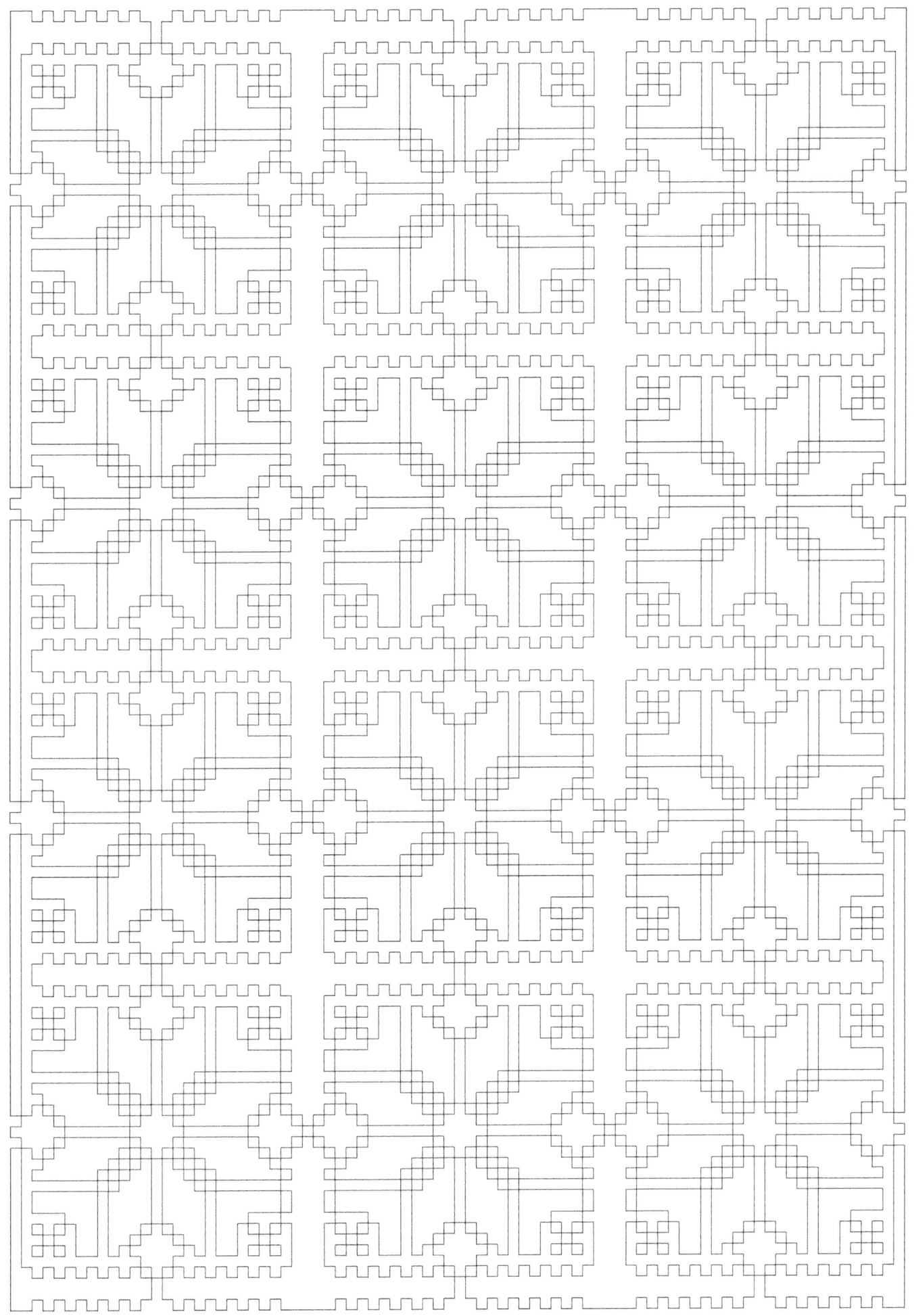

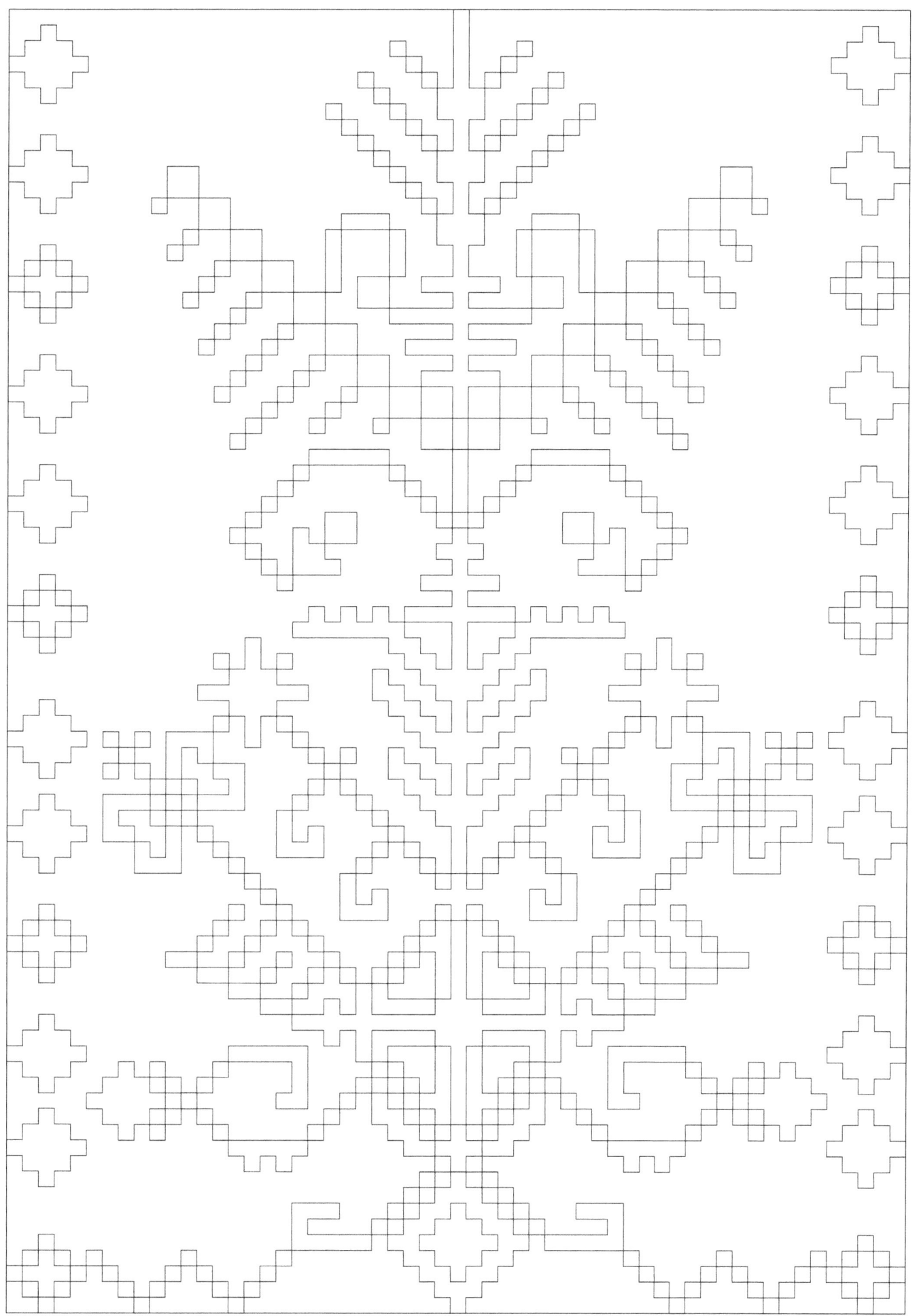

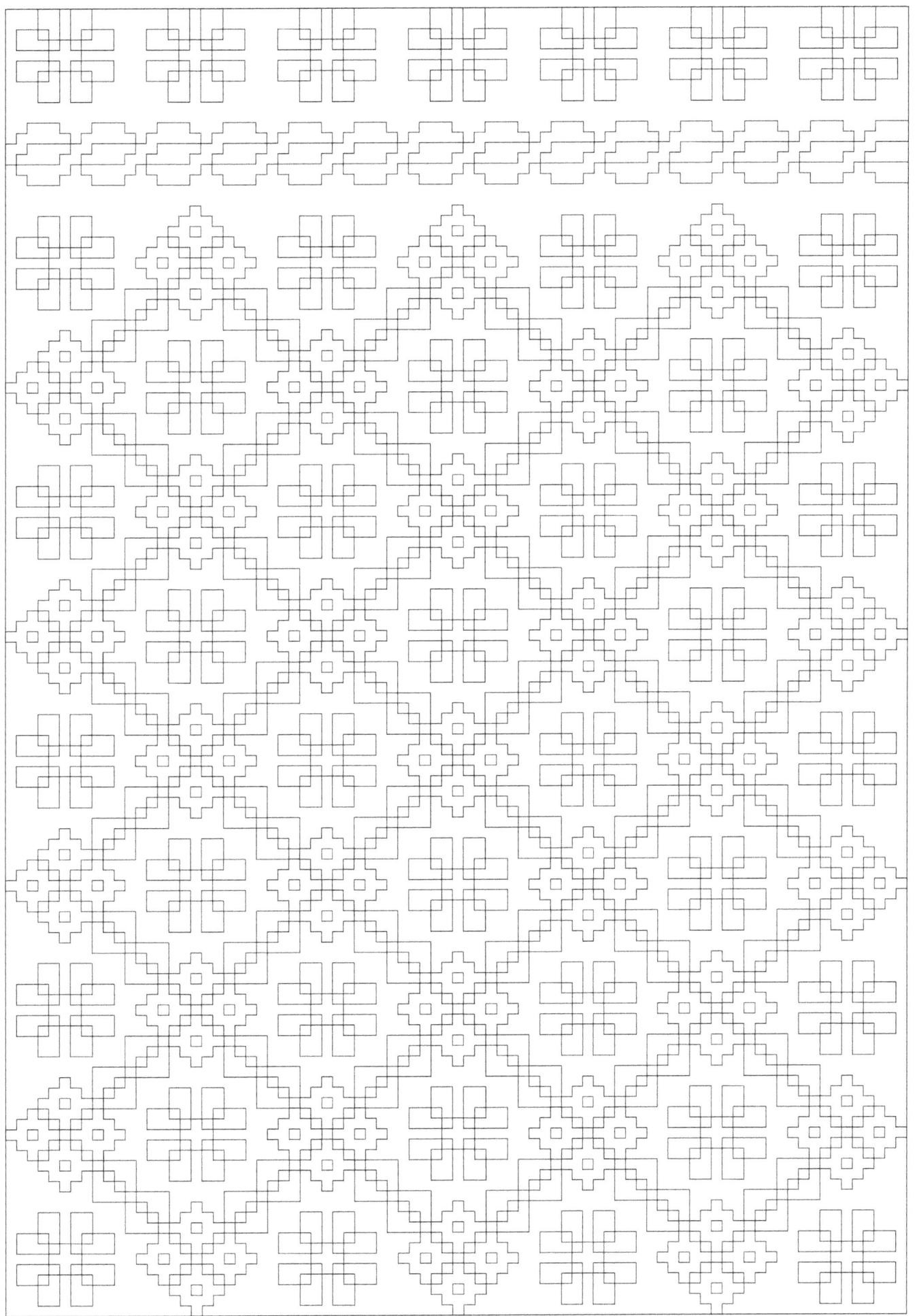

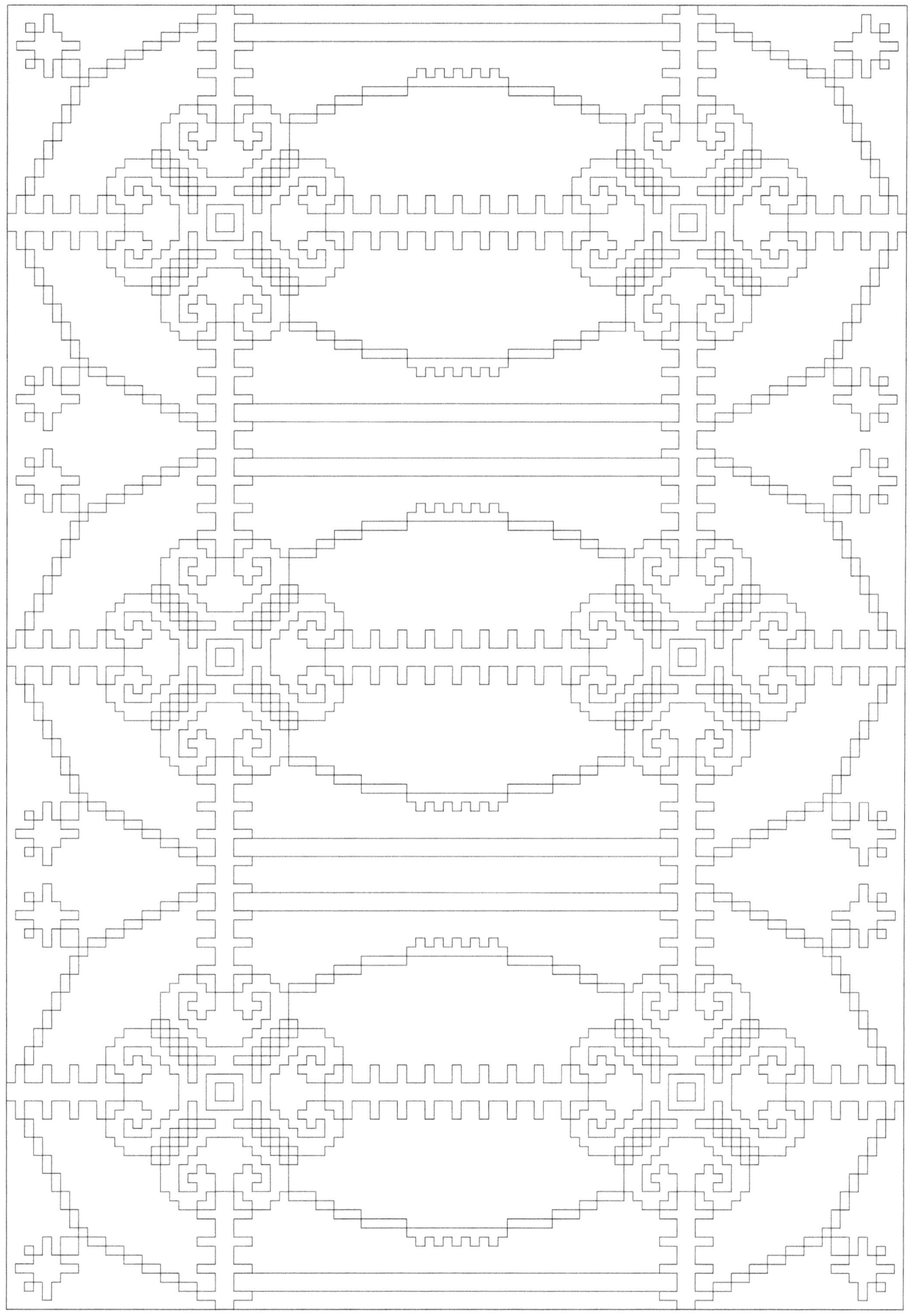

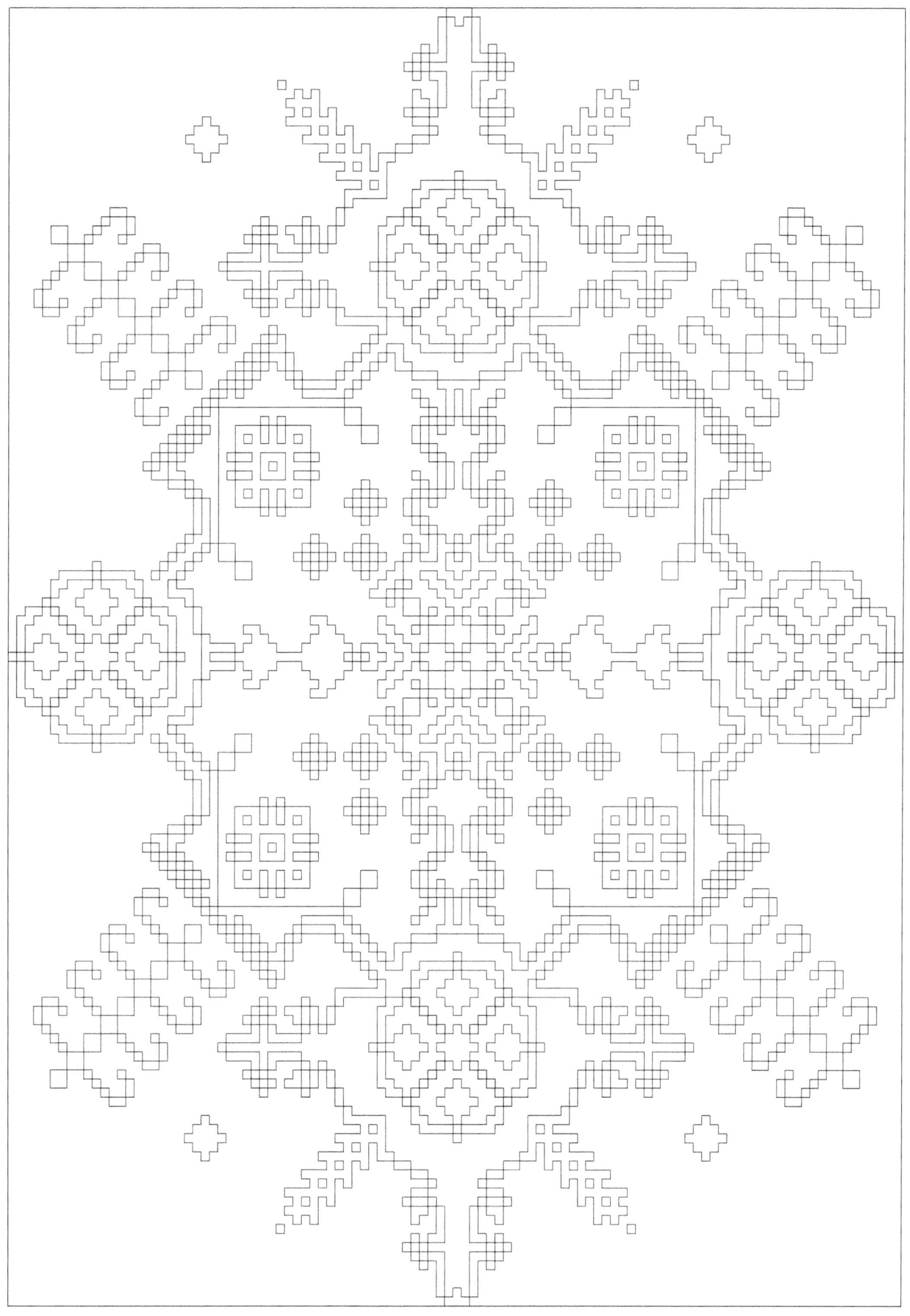

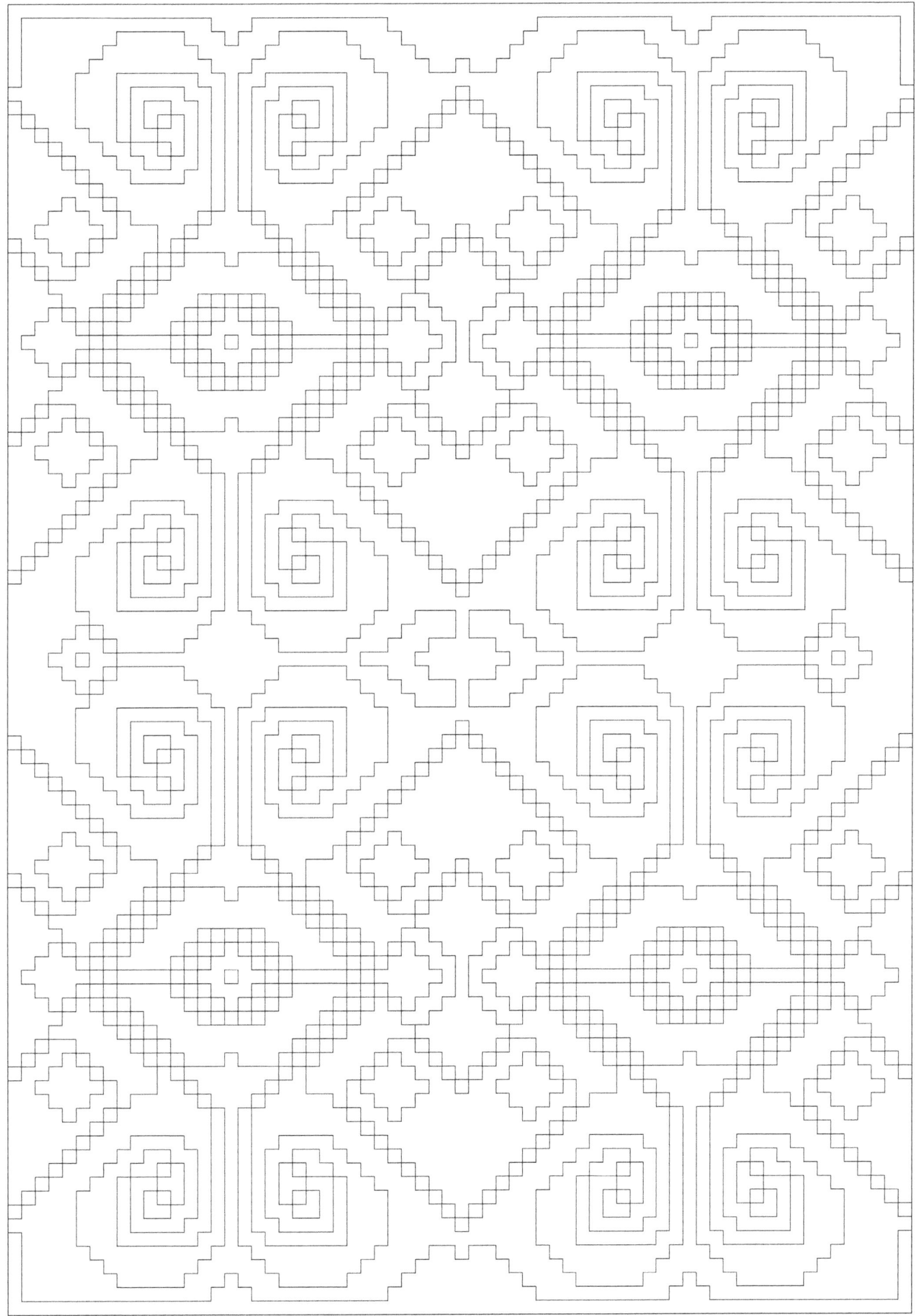

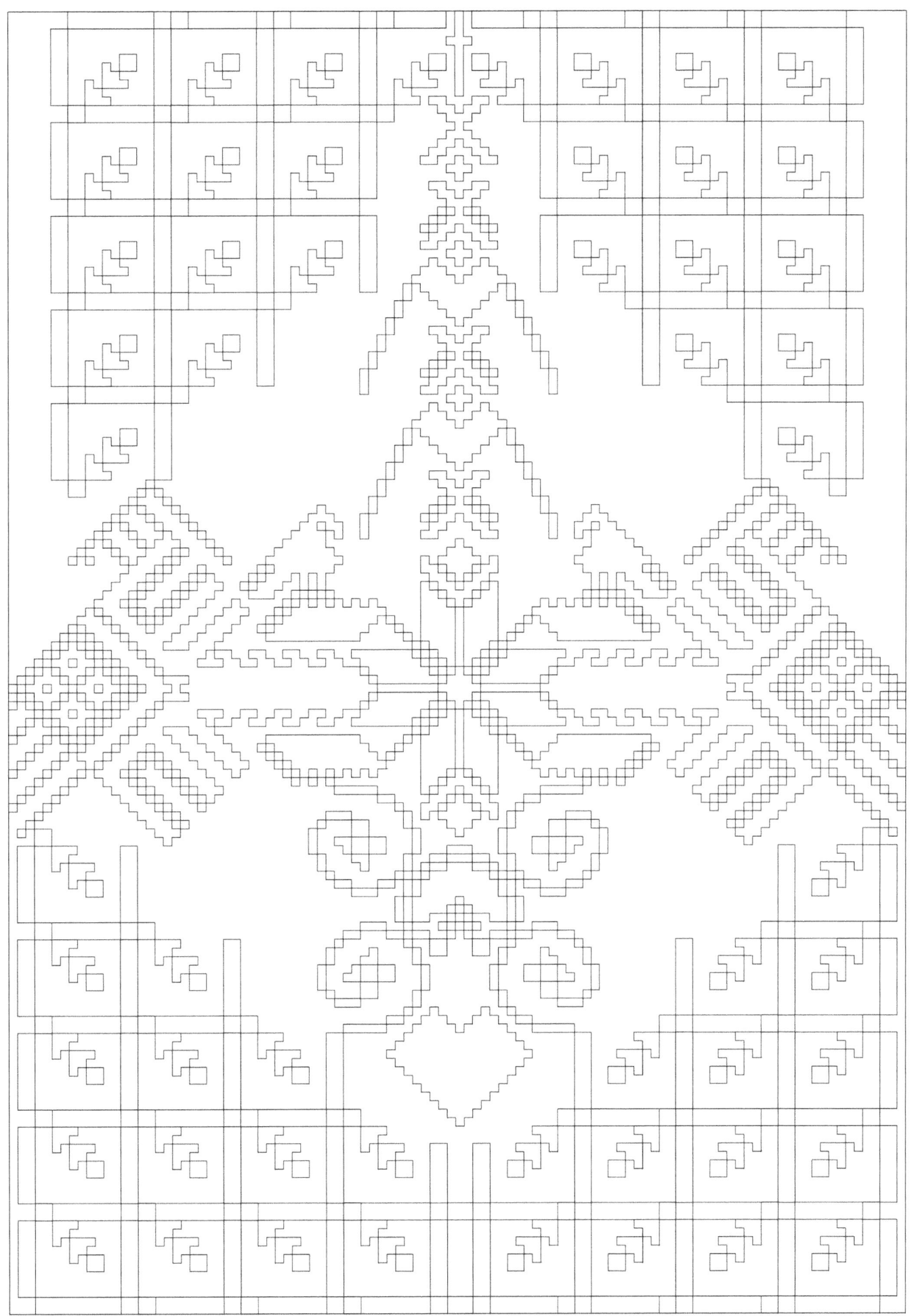

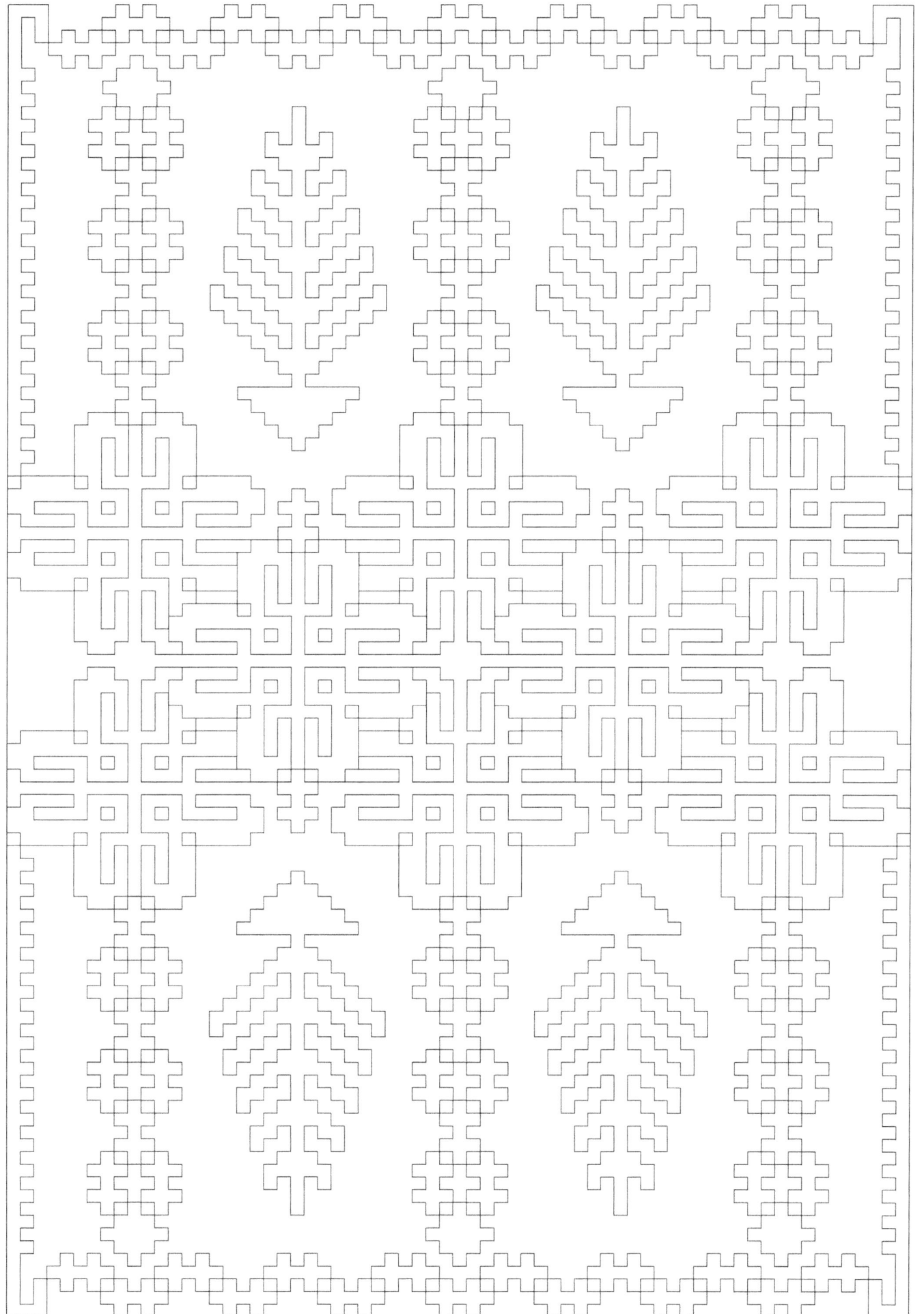

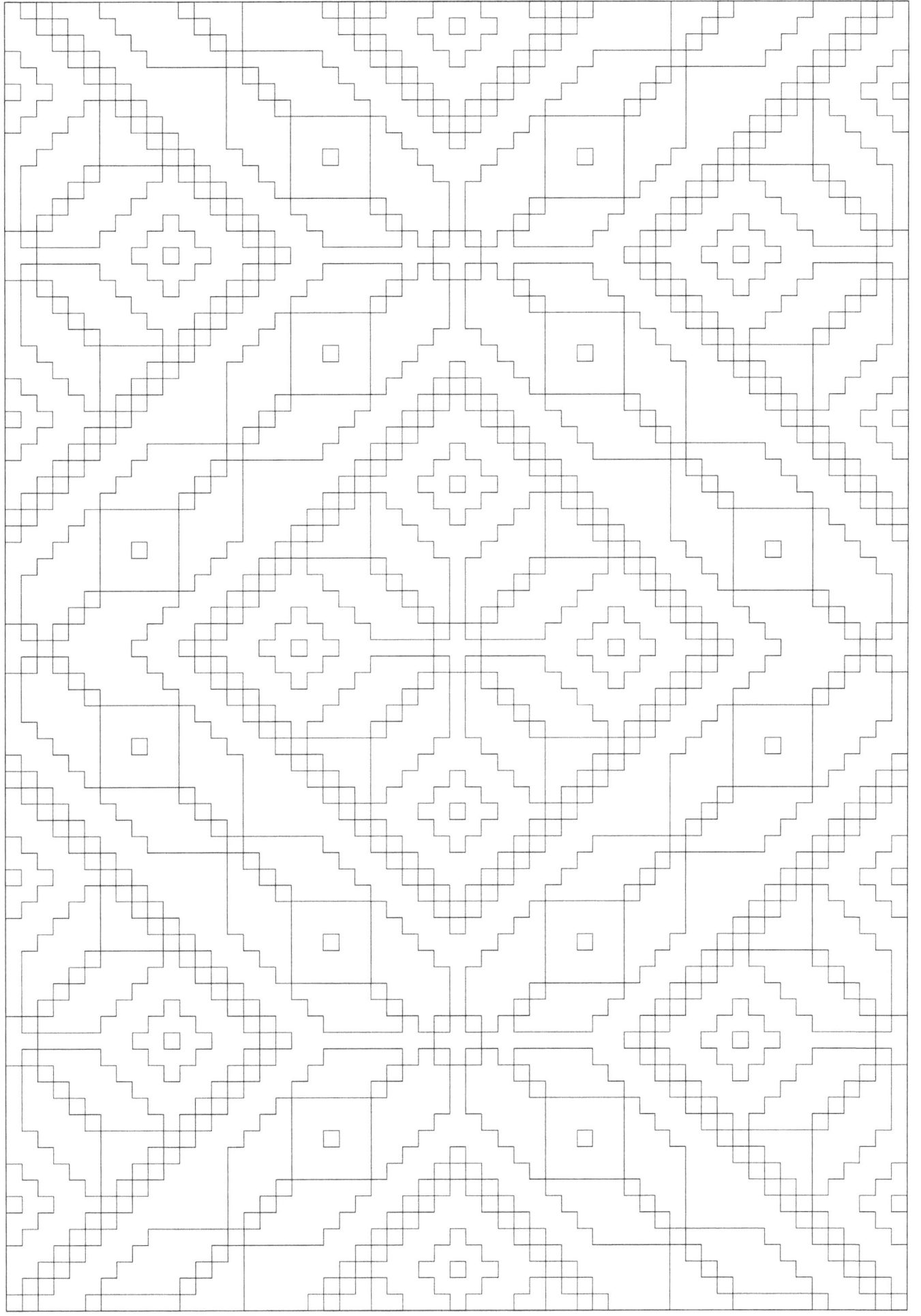

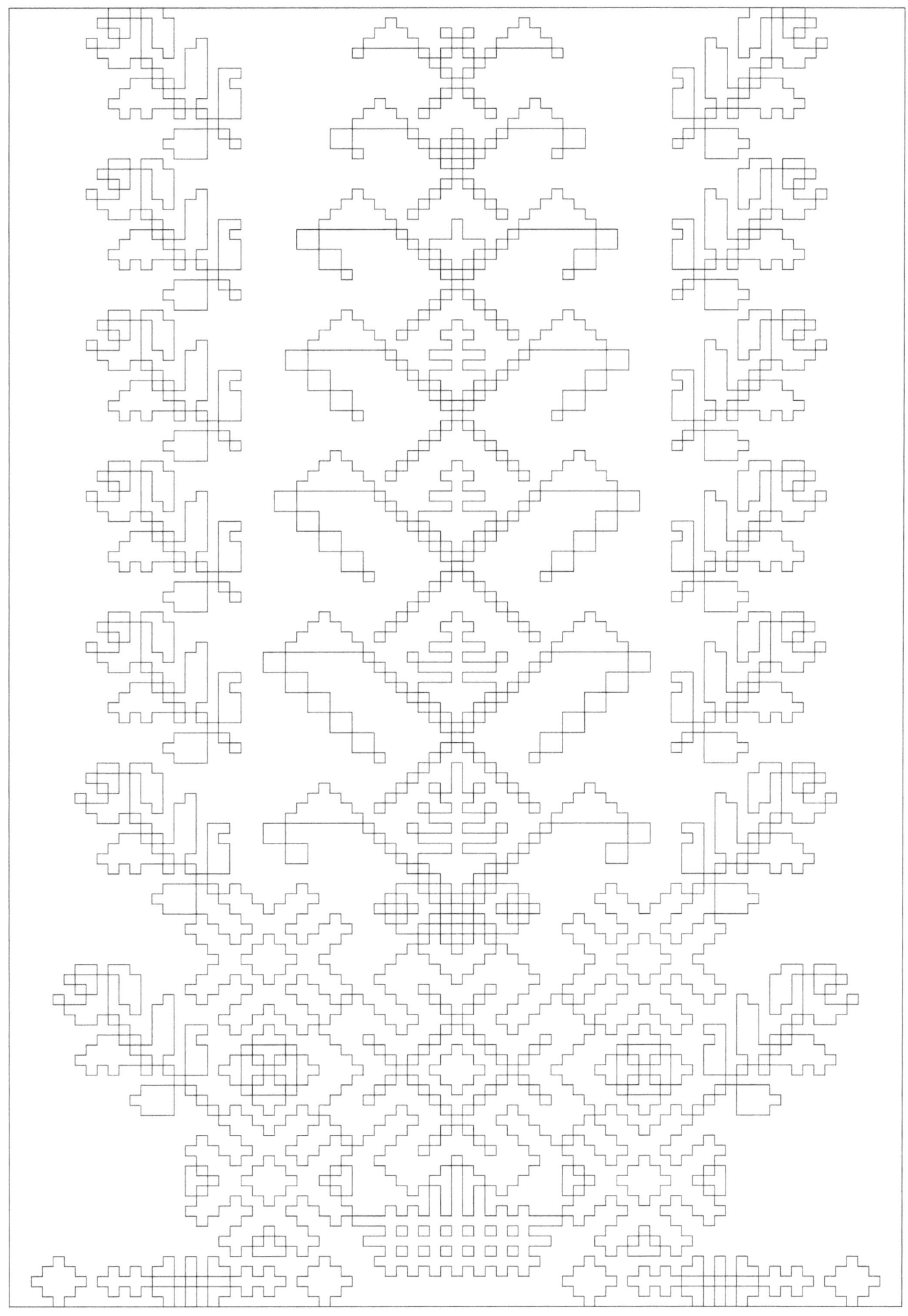

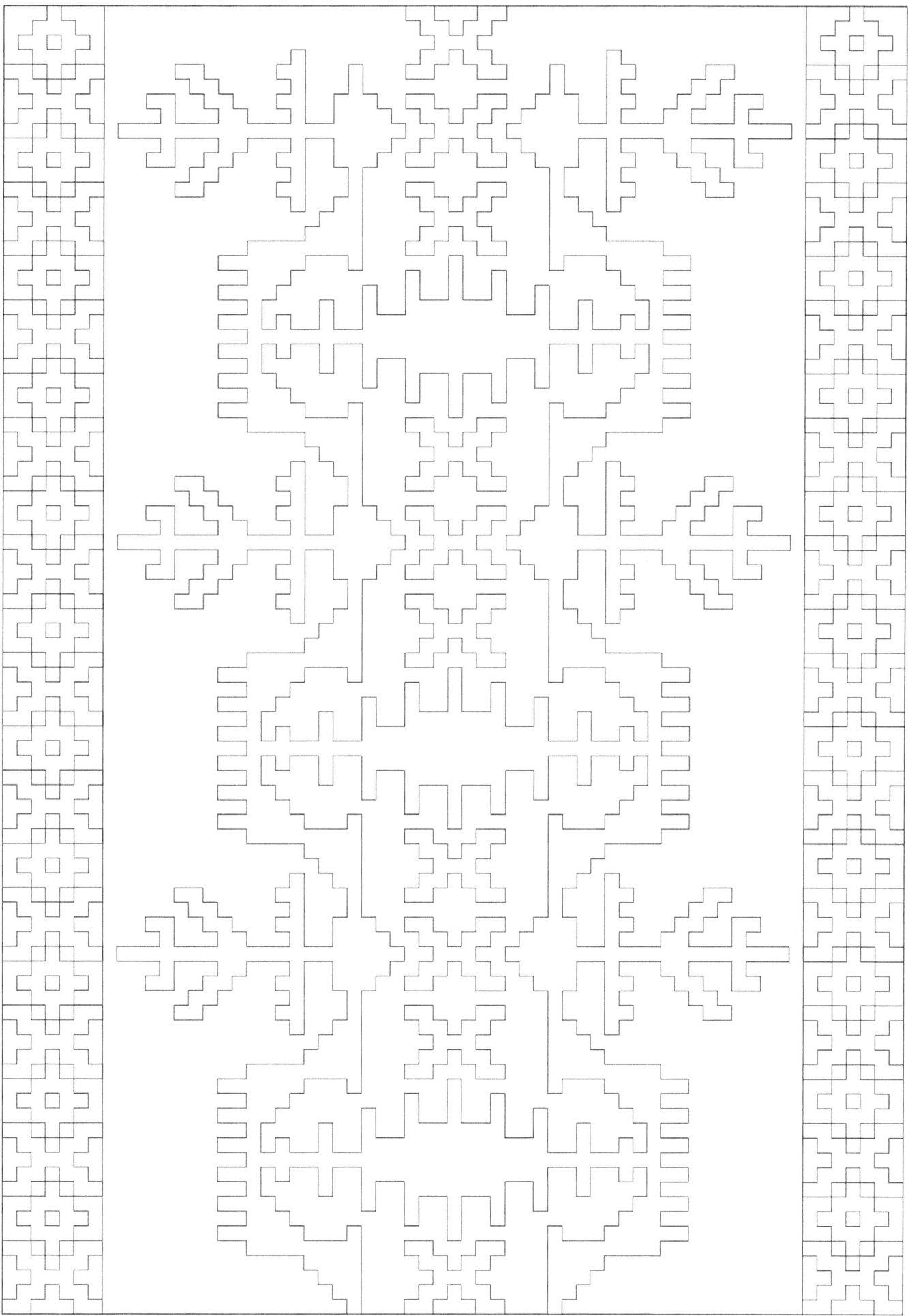

.

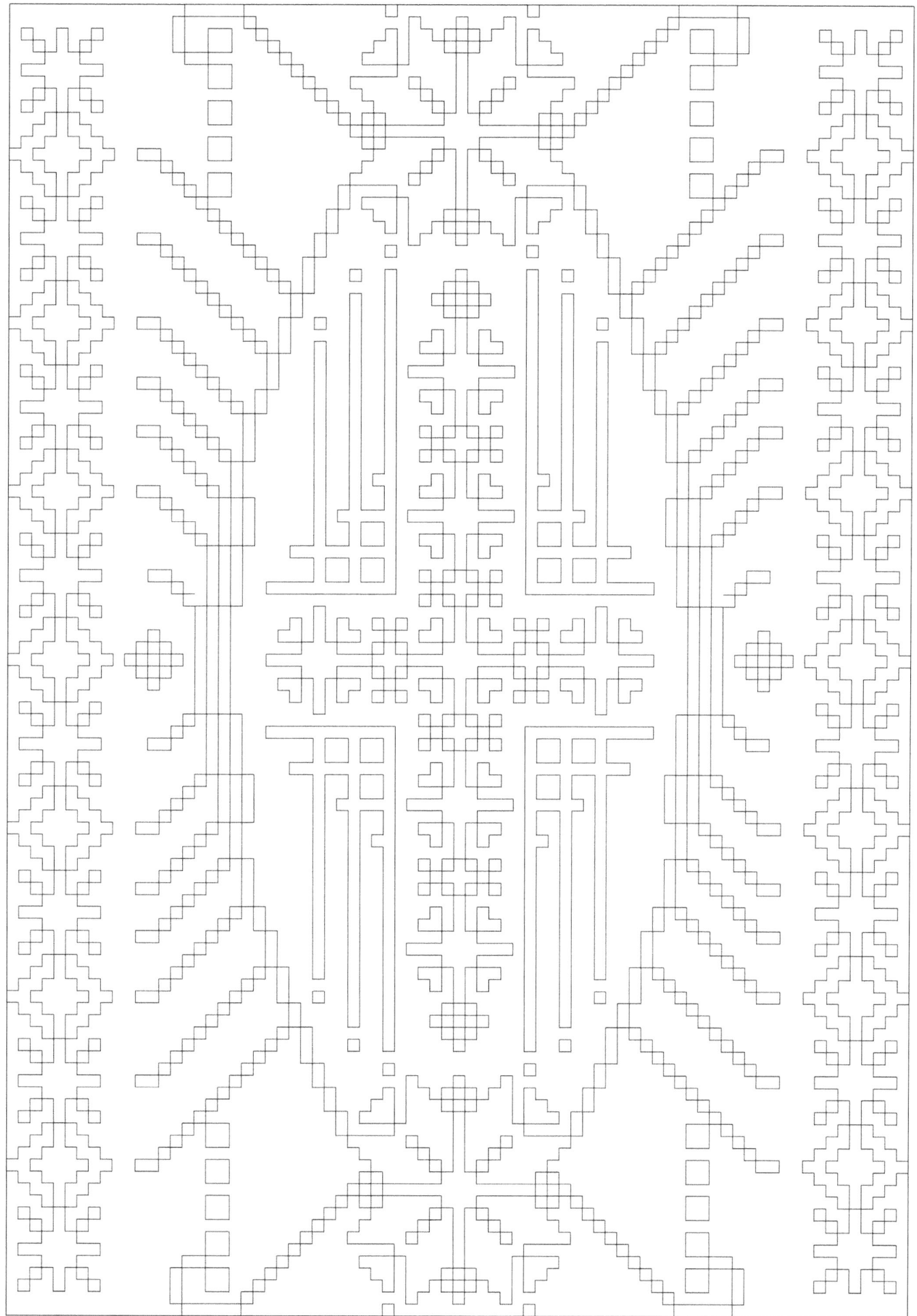

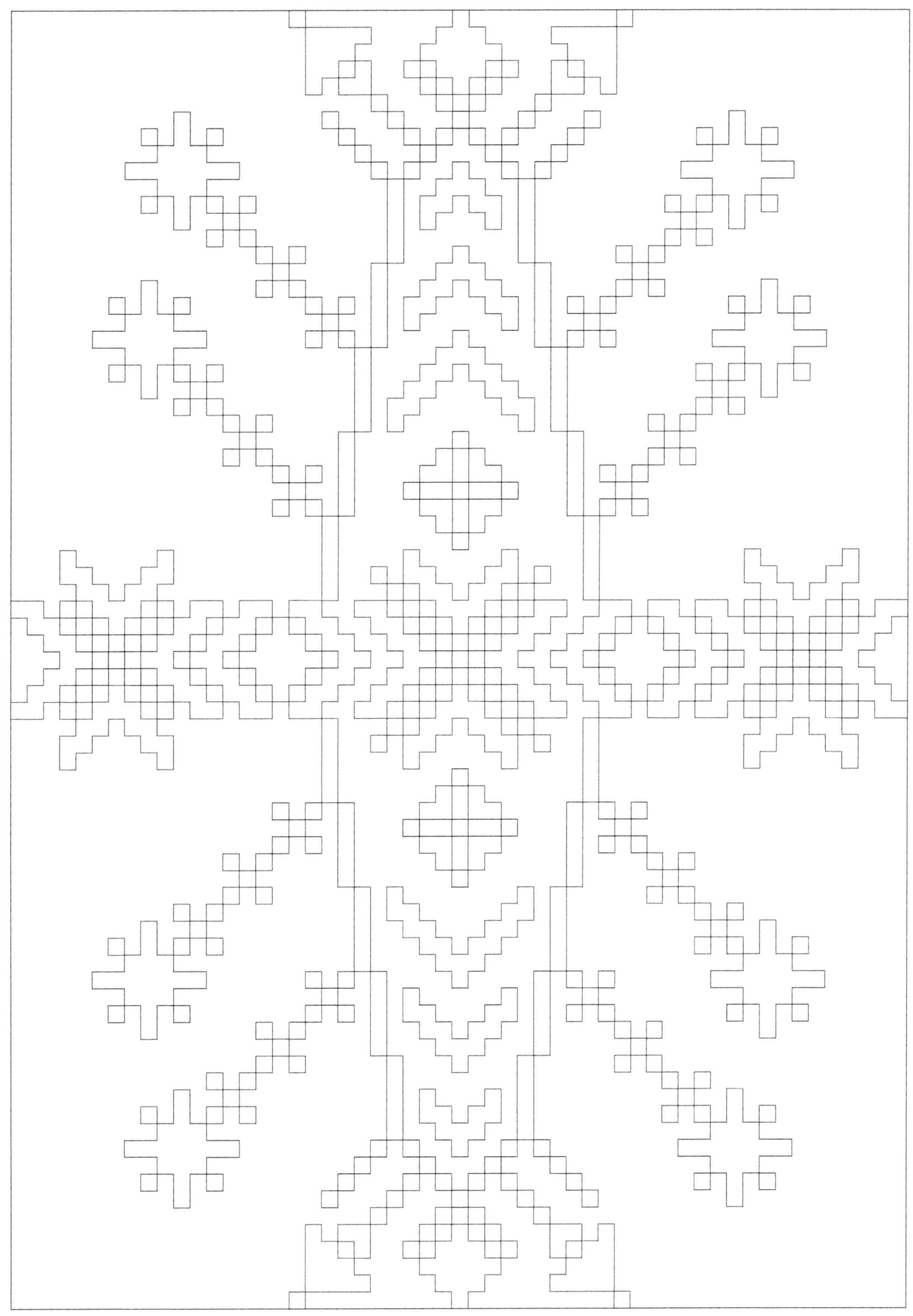

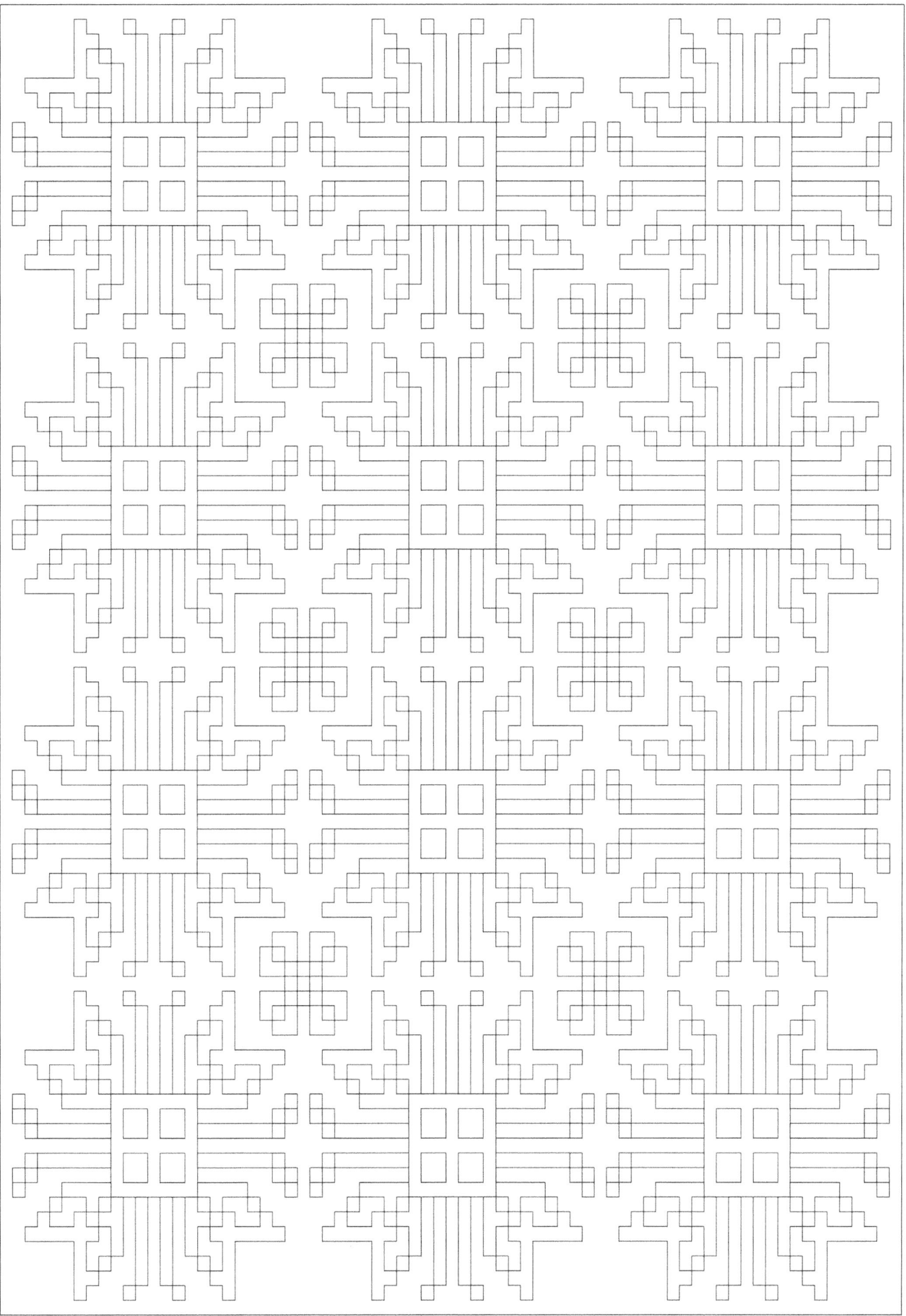

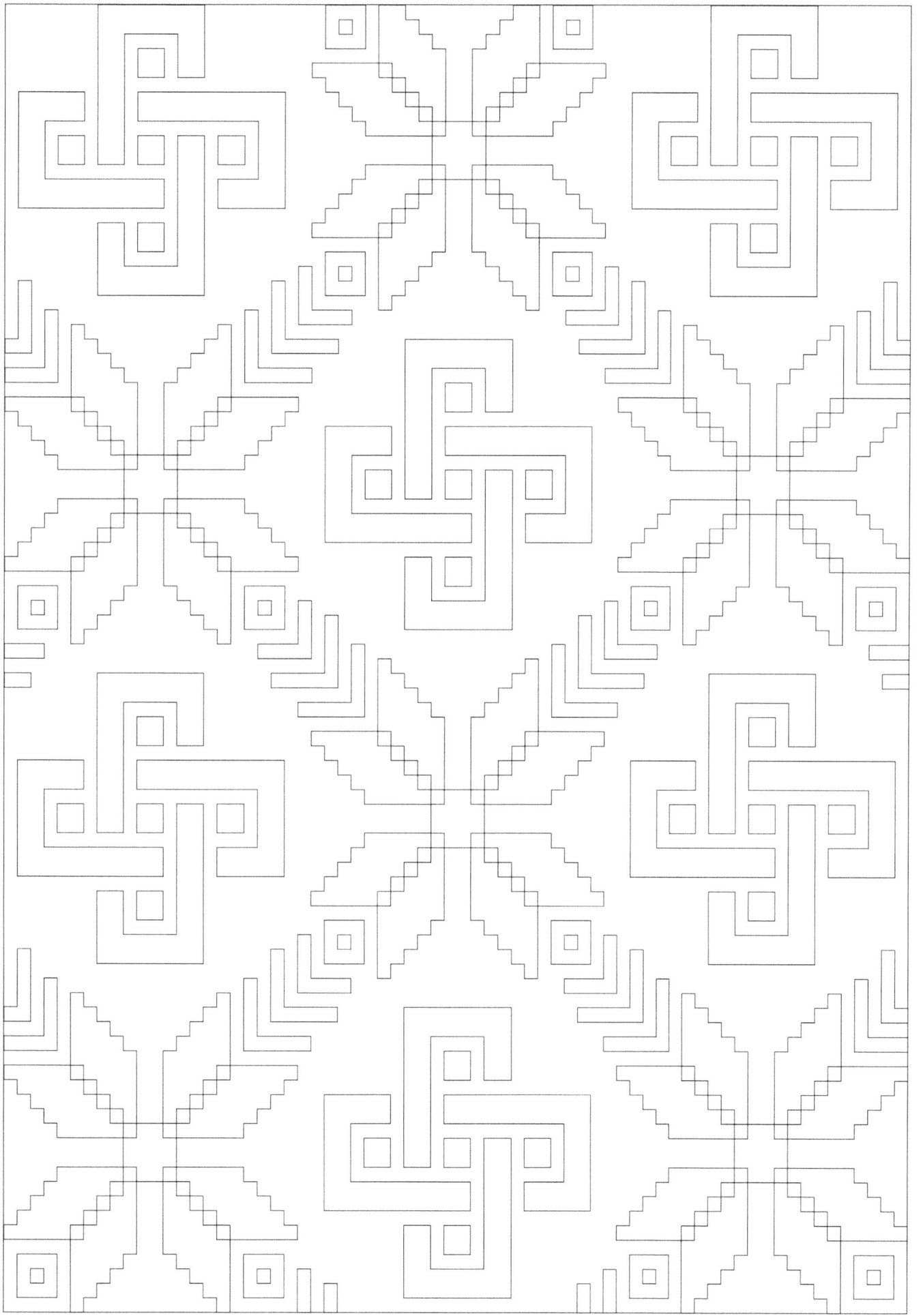

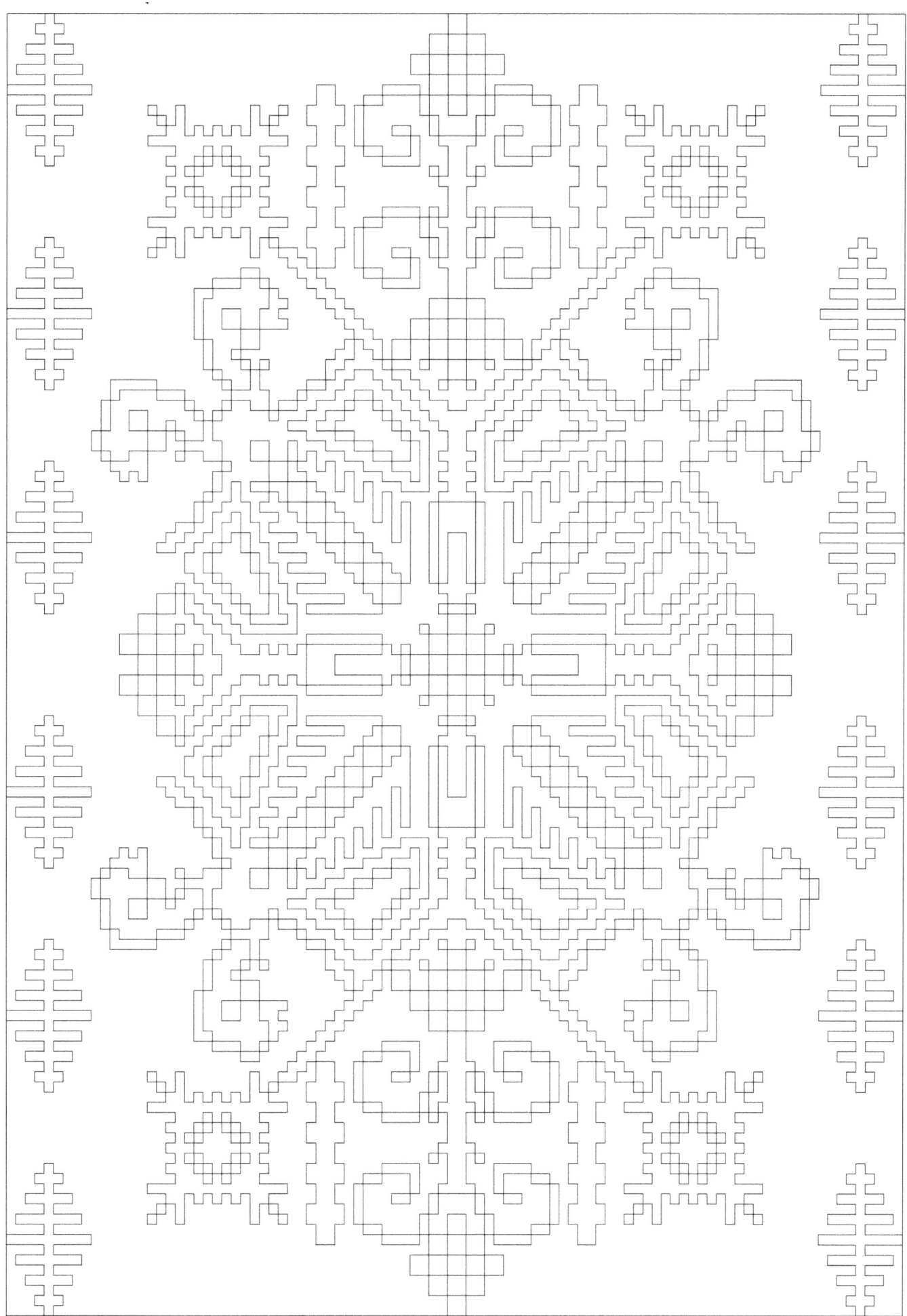

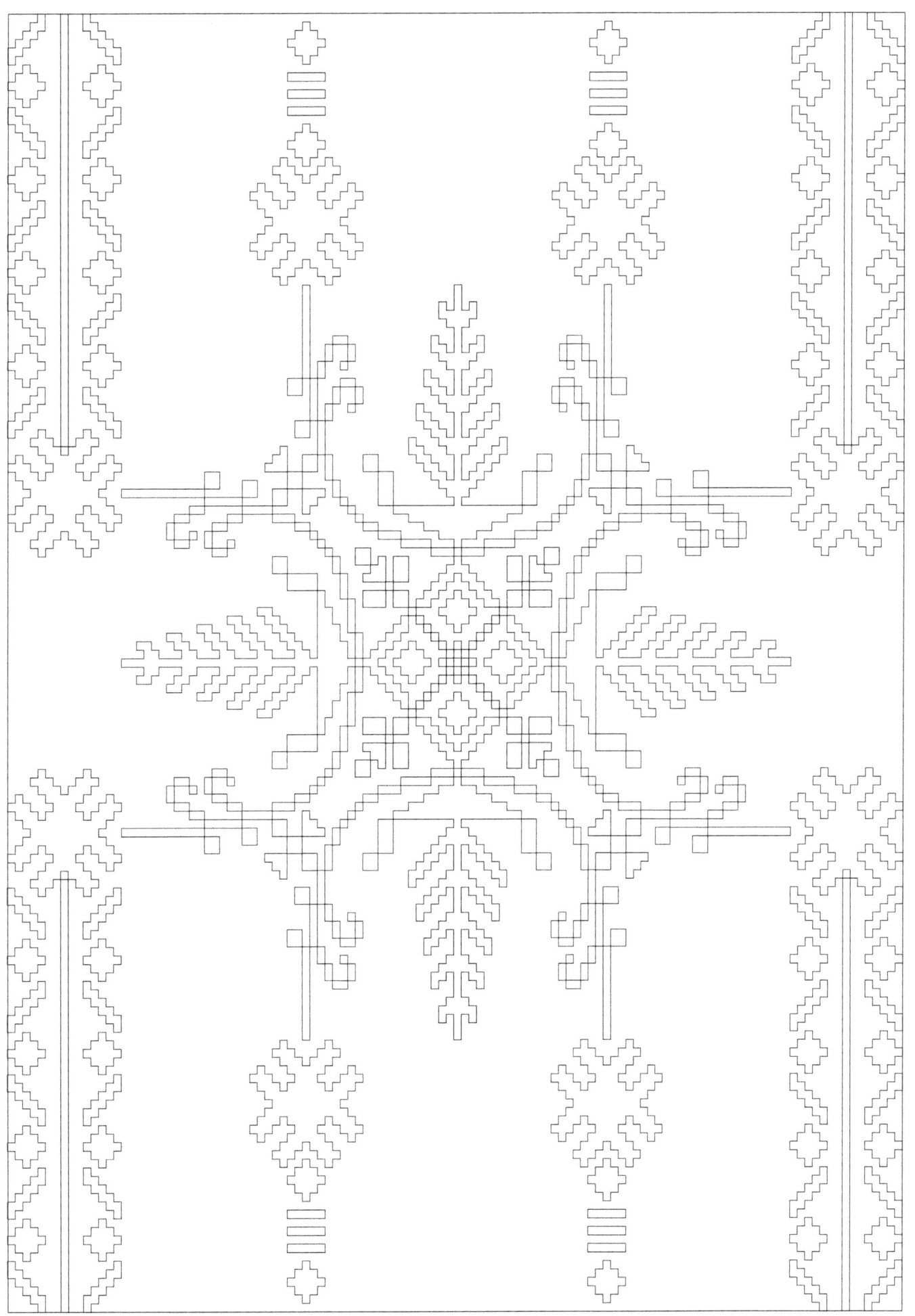

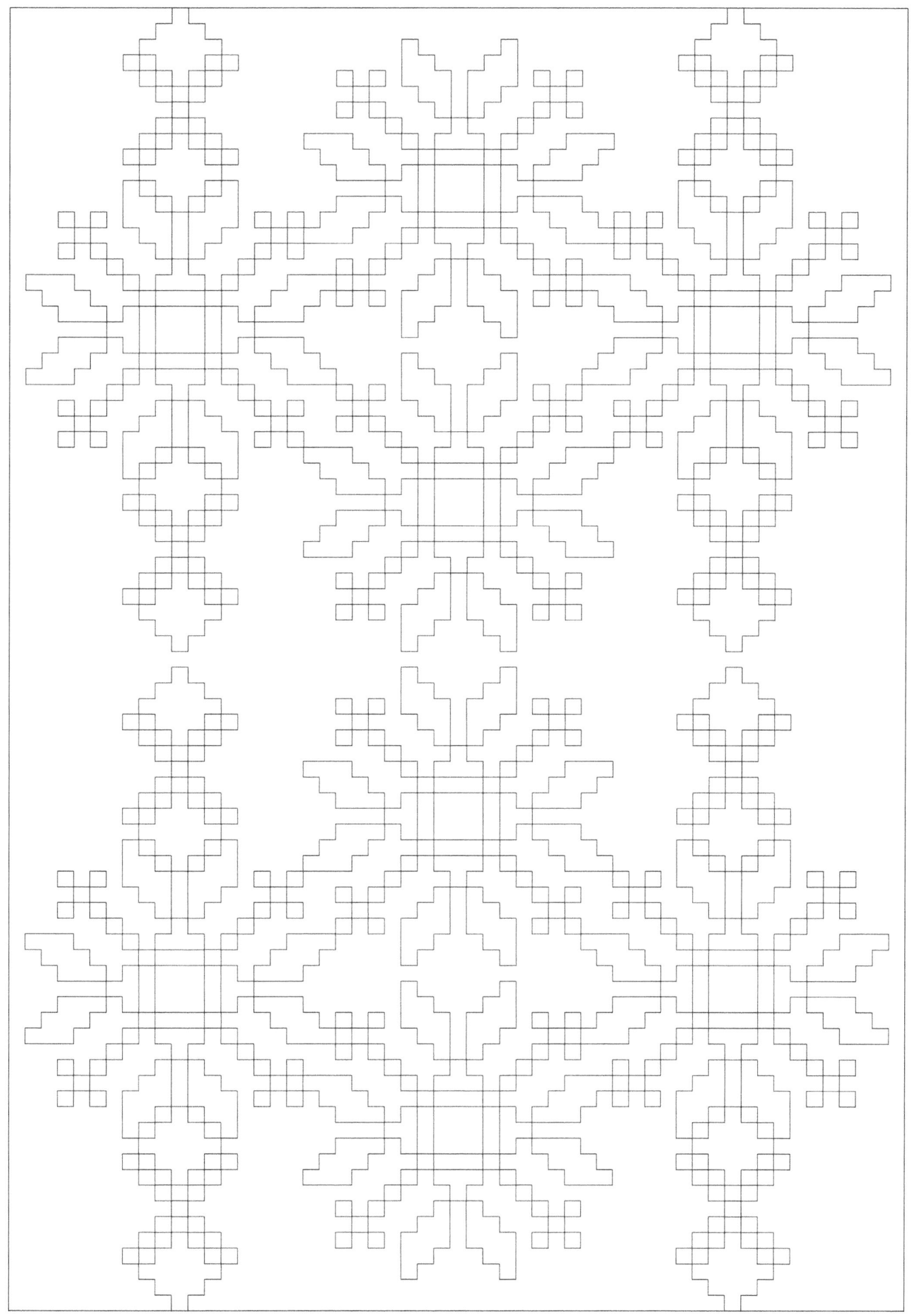

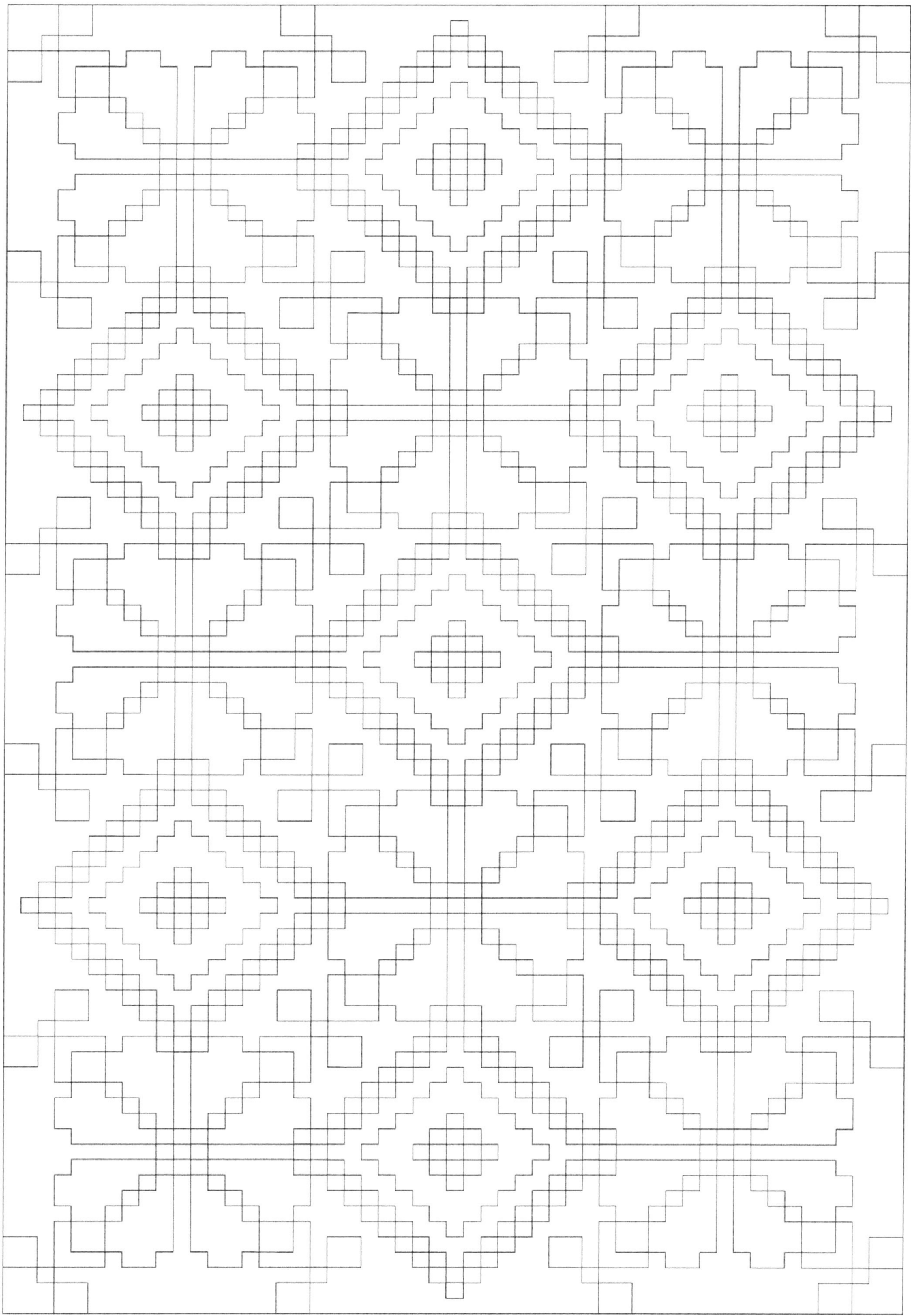

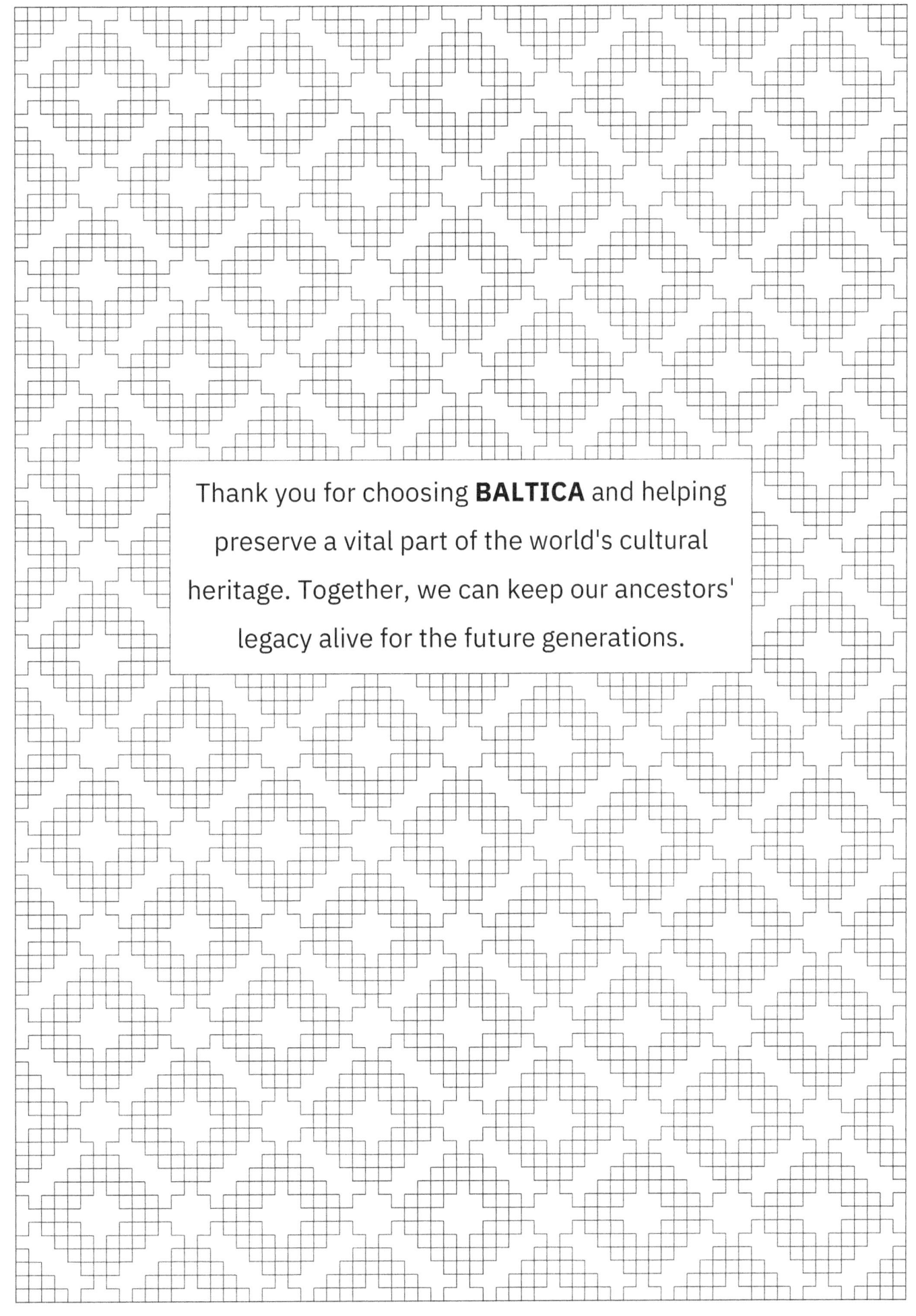

Thank you for choosing **BALTICA** and helping preserve a vital part of the world's cultural heritage. Together, we can keep our ancestors' legacy alive for the future generations.